Nature's Box of Love and Wisdom.

Mari Miller

Contents

PART ONE
GAEA: GODDESS OF EARTH   1

    A Tree Usurped   3
    What is it?   4
    Because I Stopped to Listen   5
    Winter Scenes Seen Through My Bedroom Window   6
    Penitence   7
    Walking the Dog on a Winter Day   8
    The Young Buck   9
    Spring Scenes Seen Through My Kitchen Window   11
    The Tulip   12
    Summer Scenes Seen Through My Living Room Window   13
    Solvitur Ambulando Abandoned   14
    The Hike   15
    Fallen Leaves   18
    Prairie Pumpkin   19
    The Last Bloom   22
    Trust   23
    What Would Thoreau Think About Walking Today?   24

PART TWO
PANDORA: FIRST WOMAN or
30 MINUTES OF INTERNET RADIO   31

    A Box   32
    Conjecture   33
    A Bottle of Time   34

A Fine Girl	35
Breeze of Summer	36
This has been going on for how long?	37
My Love's Best	38
Dreaming in California Soundbites	39
With You I Can Make IT	40
Sundown: An Original Poem by Pandora	41
Delusions	42

Part Three
APHRODITE: GODDESS OF LOVE AND BEAUTY — 53

To Botox or Not to Botox	54
Fleeting Moments	55
Wink at the Moon	56
The "C" Word	58
Of Love and Like	59
The Brave and His Bride	60
Seasoned Encounters	61
I Thought About You Less Today	62
Forego or Reclaim	63
Excalibur	64
Vigilant	65
Ahamen Settlement	66

Part Four
ATHENA: GODDESS OF WISDOM — 71

Journals of my Youth	72
Becoming my Mother	73
Anomaly	74
What if.....	75
For You, I Wept	76
The Test	77

Adventures	78
I Blame The Walkman	79
All-Knowing	80
It's a Crying Day	81
3 of 99	82
The Crown	83
Gehenna	84

Photo Acknowledgements:
All photographs are property of the author and edited by her daughter, Madison Kyle, except for the following:

Madison Kyle – pages 3 & 7
Darci Conner – pages 13 & 81

Part One
GAEA: GODDESS OF EARTH

A Tree Usurped

A tree usurped by the river bank
Still blooms each spring
Transforms each fall.
Uprooted
Upended
Undaunted
Equal to the task.
To other trees it appears a paraplegic,
Roots dangling but not lifeless,
Differently able to do the same.

What is it?

What is it about a river
That makes me want to
Pause and run at the same time?

About a mountain
That makes me want to
Climb and bow?

About a sunset
That makes me want to
Smile and weep?

About time
That makes me want to
Stop it and speed it up?

About silence
That makes me want to
Embrace it and break it?

About questions
That makes me want to
Answer and ignore them?

Because I Stopped to Listen

Because I stopped to listen, nature spoke.

A white feather on a rainy walk told me I was on the right path.

A pine cone ancient yet new, mirroring what it is to become, encouraged me toward enlightenment.

A red-tailed hawk, dipped and soared and floated to tell me to be ready while the baby snake on the path repeated that change and healing are coming.

The grasshoppers swarmed, continually forward setting my creativity in motion.

Although I could not see them, the croaking frogs cleansed me with peace, while the whistling reeds connected me with the usefulness and purpose of all.

White birds floating like bubbles so high I feared they would burst into the Stagnant water, full of life, reminding me that movement does not always fulfill.

Lady bugs encouraging me to patiently reach for new heights and goals and blessing me with luck for both.

Monarch butterflies, only two, were enough to confirm I am on the right path to spiritual enlightenment.

Nature spoke because I stopped to listen.

Winter Scenes Seen Through My Bedroom Window

Tiny tank tracks from a herd of snowmobiles imprinted
Beside the shed whose roof has sprouted icicle-fingers
Clinging like iridescent stalactites.
A family of snow people stands watching
The snowball fight,
The snow plow's might,
And a snowfall at night
That puts a fluffy frosting so light
On the tiny tank tracks and the roof of my shed.
Quiet winter scenes seen through my bedroom window.

Penitence

Trees, heavy with the burden of ice
Bow their heads in repentance
For sins they have not committed.

Walking the Dog on a Winter Day

Snow pants first, zipped up tight
Boots on, left then right.
Neck gator, cap
Dog's still taking a nap.
Rouse her to Velcro on her coat
Clip on leash to the collar at her throat.
Time for my coat, scarf to fill the gaps
Gloves on, ready to make some laps.
One step, two step, squat and pee
Three step, four step, that's the dog, not me.
Race back toward the door
No need to do more?

Gloves off first to remove the leash.
Undo the Velcro coat of fleece.
Up the stairs she runs to take a seat
Looking down, waiting for her treat.
Scarf off me and onto the hook
Coat next with hat and gator in the sleeve's crook.
Boots off, right then left, opposite from before.
Snow pants finally, didn't I just do this chore?
Dog happy and ready to bark at passers-by
I'm exhausted as I heave a sigh.
Tired of winter's hold of ice and snow galore
That forces this ritual just to step out the door.

The Young Buck

He noticed me first.
It took me longer to see him standing, staring at me.
I said, "You're all alone?"
He looked around him as if to say, "Do you see any others?"
"Yea, me too," I whispered.
I felt honored that he would even stop to consider me.
We were two creatures, who happened upon each other in the silent ravine,
Yet grateful to have our existences acknowledged.

He tired of me first.
He turned, flipped his white tail and bounded gracefully over fallen, snow-covered trees.
I turned, adjusted my stocking cap and trudged clumsily through shin-deep snow.
The connection had passed, but I felt warmed by our momentary bond.
Struggling up the hillside, I paused to survey my surroundings.
I saw him farther ahead of me, looking down at my progress.
Again, he was off with the flirt of a tail.
"Don't worry," I said. "I'm going off this way. I won't follow you anymore."

By the time I neared the top, he was standing next to the roadside.
I could hear a vehicle approaching, and I feared he would flip and flirt right into its path.
I whistled.
He paused.
The car passed.
He crossed.
I finished my ascension and walked down the road.
To my left he walked through the prairie grass.

I stopped to sit on a swing overlooking the ravine.

When I turned to continue, I saw him paused and
Realized his parallel path was leading him
To the security of friends and family.
Yet as he joined them, he remained apart
Even as my path took me farther away I could distinguish him.
I waved.
He bowed.

Spring Scenes Seen Through My Kitchen Window

The winds of spring are the lion's roar,
Lifting leaves into a ferocious funnel.
Robins return for the final trilogy of snow.
Newspapers flee free from readers' hands.
Here comes an empty popcorn tub,
Discarded after family movie night.
The lion is fierce today!
Swings sway back-and-forth, back-and forth,
Waiting for the weight of a child to steady it.
There goes a piece of plastic,
No longer needed to shield windows from the lion's icy cousin.
Thank you, Lion, for tossing my hair, flying my kite, and
Whipping-up spring scenes seen through my kitchen window.

The Tulip

Why does she keep cutting me down?
Every time I push my way through all the crap, she's right there to mow me over.
That's it.
I've had enough.
I'm not going to do it anymore.
I don't need this shit.
I was just trying to liven-up the landscape with some color, to be that splash of yellow in a sea of green.
I don't think she understands what I go through.
Waiting and waiting.
For months and months, I wait until all the elements are in place for me to make an appearance.
I don't push through with a huge fanfare and a loud "Ta-dah!"
I just inch my way up and out.
Then as soon as I start budding, she's there, racing and roaring, sucking me up and spitting me out.
I just can't do it anymore.
It's too hard.
I don't think I have it in me to keep trying.
I'll retreat within, like always.
I have no choice.
I'll wait, and I'll hope, and I'll plan that next time it will be different.
Next time she'll let me be.
Next time she'll let me do what I was destined.

Summer Scenes Seen Through My Living Room Window

Squirrels frolic and flit, wrestling for fun and a well-deserved break.
Ferns unfurled to catch the warmth of the sun.
A sparrow perches on the bird bath's rim, his head twitching from side-to-side.
The fullness of the red maple's leaves hides my view of the street
Until I crouch to see through my dog's eyes
Swimsuit-clad children racing to the coolness of the pool.
The pink poppies have popped wide, saluting visitors and passersby.
The bumblebee is begging me to join in these
Buzzing summer scenes seen through my living room window.

Solvitur Ambulando Abandoned

My confidante, you have betrayed me.
My muse, you have abandoned me.
My soul mate, you have forsaken me.

Traversing briefly down your path,
Your instruments of spite force me back.
Your stinging sentries stationed to halt my advance.

The Hike

The sentinel keeps the hill from sliding toward the ravine,
And gives me a hand-hold to steady myself on the descent.
Scarred and broken, she still stands strong.
I continue downward, glancing back to say,
"Thank you."
A labyrinth of logs await,
Fallen to test my resolve.

Another sentinel, his head decapitated by wind or illness,
Has at the base of his trunk, shavings that carpet the earth.
Refuse of the creature who calls the headless hull its home.
I reach the creek bed, a mere trickle.
Choosing to clamber over rocks instead of trees,
My pace quickens, my eyes dart to where my feet are to follow.
No longer looking at the woods around me,
My mission is to follow one rock to the next, playing
A game to avoid soaked socks.

An impasse.
Pause on a rock to take a drink of water from my thermos.
"Nothing personal," I say to the stream.
Chart my course over the deeper, wider, faster waters.
A mosquito distracts me or guides me, not sure which.
I stop to listen, but my mind races as fast as its wings.
I need a translator.
"If you're going to tag along," I tell it, "ride on my hat and keep quiet."

Two small saplings serve as hand-holds while I once again ascend.
A snake-like vine, reminiscent of Jumanji, has strangled a tree,
And lost its life in the process.
Baby steps now as I follow a trail downward.

A yellow-tipped butterfly glides gracefully without need
Of traction or hand-holds.
The trail is temporarily lost as leaf 5047 joins her sisters on the floor.
A baby pine has been mauled, its tendrils surrounding the scar.
The rut has begun.
That explains why that doe stared at me as if I were competition.

The vegetation grows dense and just when my claustrophobia threatens,
I come to a clearing and a fence line.
The harvest hasn't begun here yet.
The blue, bulbous water tower helps me collect my bearings.
The mosquito speaks no more,
But the rising welt behind my ear speaks volumes.
I've seen that tree before, that rock looks familiar.
Panic creeps low in my gut.
I'm like a horrid power point that just keeps looping.

A bridge.
I know that bridge.
Just beyond that bridge is a steep path that will take me to
Almost exactly where I left the scooter.
Stop on the bridge to gather strength
And a few more sips of water.
Again, nothing personal.

No way to zigzag
The trail is vertical.
The wind offers me encouragement
Or maybe a swift kick.
A white arrow on a tree confirms my direction.
The only way out is up.

A bird laughs at me while the thumping in my ears
Beats like war drums.
One last look as I catch my breath.

The mosquito's cousin just died on my elbow.
Reaching in my pocket for the scooter key,
My hand wades through the skins of civilization:
Snickers, Fruit Roll-Up, Hostess Donettes.
Other hikers before me are obviously illiterate.

Fallen Leaves

Fallen leaves look prettier
In someone else's yard.
Especially
When they've blown there from mine.

The blood red leaves of my maple
Give my neighbor's lawn a
Fiery glow in the noon time sun, but
Apparently he doesn't enjoy the view
Outside his window
As much as I do from mine.

For every day his mower moans,
Chops, grinds and spits
Precisely
When I'm lying down for a nap.

Prairie Pumpkin

It was just lying there amidst the tall, drying prairie grass.
I had scolded my dog for taking us on this route,
But apparently she knew fortune was waiting around the bend.
For you see the leaves were already halfway through their migration
Of creating a golden, orange-speckled shag carpet
Second only to the living room rug of my youth.
And I'd yet to traverse to my local pumpkin patch or visit Linus in his,
But it seems there was no need, for there it was
In all its round, orange glory just waiting for someone to take it home.
Perhaps it was on its way to someone's home when they were interrupted
And fearing the evidence of their pumpkin patch pilfering would reveal their guilt,
They ditched it in a ditch, expecting full well to return, under the cover of darkness to
Retrieve this fruit of their laborious yet lawless operation.

Not thinking how far into the prairie my dog had led me,
I hoisted the pumpkin onto my left shoulder.
Within a half-dozen steps, I questioned the sanity of my actions
Not because I feared the pumpkin perpetrators or the police would track me down
But because it was decidedly larger and heavier than it looked nestled on the ground.
I shifted it to my right shoulder and decided this would be a healthy addition to my walk.
From the right shoulder to the left then with both hands encircling it in front of my belly.
My dog was soon behind me undoubtedly questioning
If she too would be required to partake in this salvage mission.
Back to the left shoulder, up the incline.

Where did that hill come from?
Could this be a trap with a bomb hidden inside to send a message to future pumpkin patch villains?
I tapped the pumpkin and was amazed at how something so hollow could be so blasted heavy.

Finally the road was in sight, I shifted the pumpkin to my right shoulder,
But the car was at least another quarter of a mile.
I couldn't abandon what had just become my life's work
To give this prairie pumpkin a place of prominence on my front stoop.
Two women walked toward me.
I recognized them and searched my memory if they lived nearby and grew pumpkins.
I shifted the pumpkin to my left shoulder thinking perhaps they wouldn't notice it, but
Deciding this dodge would be fruitless, I thought fast and brilliantly spouted,
"Apparently the prairie is producing pumpkins this year."
They politely chuckled at the silliness of a
Fifty-something woman toting a ten-pound pumpkin in the middle of a state park
While a 10-pound pup sheepishly followed 10 paces behind.
Perhaps I should've rolled the pumpkin and carried the pup.

Finally around the curve, the final leg.
That little engine had nothing on me.
Balancing the prairie's pumpkin on a numbed left shoulder, I
Unlocked the car and lifted the hatch to place the sadistic sphere
Ceremoniously, triumphantly albeit discreetly out of sight.
Pausing to catch my breath, I gave a sardonic, Grinchesque smile as I
Delighted in my prairie pumpkin caper.
The original thief would have a big surprise to
Find his future jack-o-lantern had sprouted legs and run away.
Safely home and under the cover of near darkness, I hoisted that
Pumpkin once more, but not by its belly or its bottom.

Despite carrying this pumpkin for nearly a mile, I forgot the first rule of pumpkin toting.

In disbelief I stared at the stem in my hand as the pumpkin crashed to the ground.

The Last Bloom

I pass your window.
Your face withers without the sun.
Your head bows beneath the weight of the frost.
Your arms droop deeply toward the ground.

Within minutes, I pass you again.
Your face disappeared during my absence.
Your head shrank, ashamed.
Your arms removed, defeated.

Trust

"I don't wanna."
"It's okay. I'll catch you."
"I don't wanna."
"It's alright. I'm right here."
"I don't wanna."
"It's fine. I'm a soft landing."
"I don't wanna."
"It's safe. Look at all the others down here who've done it."
"I don't.....you always said, 'If your friends jumped off a bridge, would you'?"
"I know, but this is different."
"That's 'cause this is a tree. I don't wanna."
"Then I guess you'll be all alone up there."
"I don't.....whadya mean, *alone*?"
"We'll all be snug and warm, huddled together down here."
"Alone? Through the wind and the rain and the snow?"
"All alone. And I will miss you."
"I don't wanna.........be alone."
"Then just let yourself fall. I'll catch you."
"Here..................I................go..................wooooohhhhh................... eeeeeehhhhhhhhhhhhh!"
"Brilliantly done."
"I'm okay.
I'm alright.
I'm fine.
I'm safe.
You DID catch me, and you ARE soft.
I wanna do it again."

What Would Thoreau Think About Walking Today?

While staying at some friends' bed-and-breakfast, I happened upon Henry David Thoreau's *Walking*, a treatise on the delights of unrestrained walking and enjoying the wilder side of life. My life is currently in complete, albeit temporary, upheaval, and although I have no place at the moment to call home, wherever I go, I go for walks. I, like so many others across the last century and a half, have felt a kindred connection to Thoreau's free spirit. Often I ponder on his carefree life, which actually was not without societal constraints. Thoreau worked off-and-on in his father's pencil factory in Concord, Massachusetts. He graduated from Harvard and became a teacher, shunning the conventional teaching methods and opening a school for two years with his older brother, John. He lived with Ralph Waldo Emerson for two years as a handyman, absorbing Emerson's philosophies and borrowing a few acres of his land on Walden Pond to build a cabin from which he could walk and write. As a Transcendentalist, he believed thinking was the only way to transcend the physical world and reach the spiritual plane, and to him the best way to contemplate was while walking. He conducted a two-year experiment that shunned the typical work ethic by working one day and spending the other six in transcendental exploration. He believed in freedom for everyone, and always supported a nonviolent approach to changing inhumanities and inequalities. The farthest west he ever went was to Minnesota in an attempt to restore his health, but at age 45 he died of tuberculosis. *Walking* began as a lecture and was finally published in *The Atlantic* a month after his death. It wasn't until reading Thoreau's treatise, however, that I actually thought about the act, even the art, of walking and what he would think of the walking we do today.

He begins his essay by offering possible definitions of *sauntering*, which he says may be derived from people in the Middle Ages who went about the countryside asking for alms while on their trek to *a la Sainte Terre*, the Holy Land. As Thoreau said, "... the children exclaimed, 'There goes a *Sainte-Terrer*, a Saunterer,' — a Holy-Lander." (p. 1). Few people in the 21st century use the word saunter, probably because our contemporary definition has more to do with laziness and a general lacking of direction and purpose. People who saunter through life do not amount to anything. Right? Thoreau would disagree. He would be dismayed at our lack of meandering. Even in his own time he chastised his fellow men that, "Half the walk is but retracing our steps" (p. 6). To have a destination, route, or time-frame is not a leisurely stroll but rather an organized, purposeful movement. Often my walking takes me to beautiful woods and prairies, my own personal Holy Land, where I am inspired to write on the beauty of nature and solitude and reflect upon my relationships with nature and with humans. I think Thoreau would approve.

I have no plans for where I will begin or where I will end my walks, aside from needing to be in somewhat close proximity to the vehicle that brought me or the abode in which I reside. "Our expeditions are but tours, and come round again at evening to the old hearth-side from which we set out" (p. 6). It is as if he were describing our walking habits today rather than more than a century-and-a-half ago, however, he too started from his home and returned to it. I think he was chastising his own lack of motivation and ambition as well as that of his peers. "Some of my townsmen it is true, can remember and have described to me some walks which they took ten years ago, in which they were so blessed as to lose themselves for half an hour in the woods, but I know very well that they have confined themselves to the highway ever since,...." (p. 8). I think it's the fear of having lost themselves both spiritually and physically that prevented them from taking to the woods again. To be lost means to have no direction and while my personal and professional life require direction and purpose, when walking, my sauntering mind matches my sauntering limbs. Becoming lost suits the person who saunters. We are so afraid of losing ourselves, both in the woods and in our minds, for surely one begets the other. "I am alarmed when it happens that I have walked a mile into the woods bodily, without getting there in spirit." (p. 13)

I took to the woods at an early age, walking four blocks from home, crossing railroad tracks, skirting a pond, and sauntering down a cow path to reach pastures and trees, both fallen and standing, and a creek that varied in size according to the season. I do not recall having a destination, and my only purpose was to be alone and to avoid cow pies. I was unencumbered. No deadlines or responsibilities beyond that of getting home in time for supper. I walked. I observed. Thoreau would have approved as this type of walking was wild and free. "Life consists with wildness. The most alive is the wildest" (p. 33). If I think really hard, I can recall that wildness. Wildness in nature, not normally in me. I was not a wild child so going to the woods allowed me to break free from the inevitable expectations that even an adolescent must face. I sauntered back in those days because I had not a care in the world and cared not if the world thought me a meanderer. Not so the walking of my adulthood where commitments demand directed and purposeful walking. I doubt Thoreau would agree, but he certainly would understand.

I believe Thoreau preferred to walk west or southwest because during his time the West was synonymous with wildness and growth. "The West of which I speak is but another name for the Wild; and what I have been preparing to say is that in Wildness is the preservation of the World." (p. 30) What would he think now that going west no longer affords wildness no matter how wild one might consider California. Personally, I stereotype the western part of the United States as more free and open and the eastern part as more reserved and sophisticated. "We go eastward to realize history and study the works of art and literature, retracing the steps of the race; we go westward as into the future, with a spirit of enterprise and adventure." (p. 22). This notion of wildness plays heavily into Thoreau's treatise, and I agree that I feel my most free when walking in the woods. The silence encourages my thoughts. The animals give me comfort. The fresh air strengthens my constitution. "For I believe that climate does thus react on man, —as there is something in the mountain-air that feeds the spirit and inspires." (p. 28). What would Thoreau have thought or done about our current climate crisis? Undoubtedly he would have written about the criminality of humans' treatment of Earth. He would have rallied his contemporaries Emerson, Hawthorne,

Peabody, Fuller, and Mann to enlighten and educate people on the simple cause/effect relationship between poisoning our planet and poisoning ourselves. The West may yet return to the wildness of Thoreau's time as sea levels rise and a new West Coast emerges.

My wildness is not truly the wild of Thoreau's wilderness for my woods simply skirt civilization, however, his cabin on Walden Pond was just a few miles from Concord. While I have great admiration for those who can live off the land by growing, fishing, and hunting for their sustenance, I know nothing of any of these skills despite being raised in Iowa. I must remain close enough to civilization to survive, but I try to locate in areas that provide a semblance of isolation and a wildnerness. What does it mean to be wild? Certainly *wild* is the antithesis of *civilization* so I can never truly be wild, but I can test the limits of acculturation. "In short, all good things are wild and free." (p. 42). I have always believed that we all need a rebellious time in our lives whether it comes at 16 or 60 for if we never shake off the shackles of conformity, we can never truly call ourselves alive. "I rejoice that horses and steers have to be broken before they can be made the slaves of men, and that men themselves have some wild oats still left to sow before they become submissive members of society." (p. 44). It is a balancing act to teach our children to observe the rules of the superego yet safeguard enough of their egos to remain freethinkers. "I love even to see the domestic animals reassert their native rights, — any evidence that they have not wholly lost their original wild habits and vigor." (p. 43). Thoreau himself lived most of his life in and around the small hamlet of Concord, and I imagine his home was similar to mine in that, while I have all the comforts of civilization, I can also escape to the wild within minutes. He does not totally shun civilization since "Nature has a place for the wild clematis as well as for the cabbage." (p. 41). Wildness and civilization can co-exist. Living in civilization yet close enough to the wild, I can easily cross the line so that walking lightens my mind, my soul, and my step. I think Thoreau would approve of my type of walking that restores, rejuvenates, revitalizes, and "When I would recreate myself, I seek the darkest wood, the thickest and most interminable, and to the citizen, most dismal swamp."

He offered another definition of sauntering that derives from "the word ... *sans terre*, without land or a home." (p. 5). Lately my walking has been related more to this second definition as I am between homes and completely dependent upon the kindness and generosity of friends and family. Although lately I rarely lay my head down in the same spot for four consecutive nights, walking remains the one constant in my temporarily, transient life. When I bunk with my younger daughter and her boyfriend, I enjoy walking the myriad of trails surrounding their apartment. Today our purposeful, destination-planned walks are on manicured trails. What would Thoreau think of all the asphalt we have lain down atop prairie grasses and shrubs? I believe he would be appalled. "Nowadays almost all man's improvements, so called, as the building of houses, and the cutting down of the forest and of all large trees, simply deform the landscape, and make it more and more tame and cheap." (p. 14). What cost will we pay for sacrificing Nature's order for Human's order? Thoreau believed in balance "When we walk, we naturally go to the fields and woods: what would become of us, if we walked only in a garden or a mall? Even some sects of philosophers have felt the necessity of importing the woods to themselves, since they did not go to the woods." (p. 12). I applaud suburban developers and chambers of commerce for creating trails because they at least get people out and about. I know Thoreau would think this a good idea too for he notes that the shopkeepers "deserve some credit for not having committed suicide long ago" (p. 9). But to walk on the safe, sturdy trails does not offer the wildness of picking one's way over fallen trees, scrambling over rocks to cross streams, and discerning a path through wilderness. I feel a satisfaction walking in the woods that I just do not feel walking on a suburban trail. However, before I consider my woods-walking too wild and free, I must note that I generally follow trails there too. Walking in the woods in my ignorant youth meant creating my own path, and then I learned that straying from the path can cause additional degradation of the landscape. I do not want to be responsible for the erosion of a hillside simply because my ego mandates I forge my own path. Following paths in the woods and prairies is more important than feeding my wild, independence. I think Thoreau the environmentalist would agree.

What would Thoreau think of all the rules some people have for walking? Proper attire apparently means name brand sportswear, Under Armour, Nike, or Adidas from top to toe. I have never been a slave to fashion trends for any activity so any walking costume will suffice, but my shoes will vary according to the terrain and the season. Snow shoes for winter trekking. Hiking boots for long jaunts and varied topography. Tennis shoes when sticking to a pathway. I am guessing that Thoreau would dress for his day the same way every day regardless of his activities and would nonchalantly rise from his breakfast table with the only thought as to whether an additional overcoat would be needed on his walk.

Another consideration we currently have for walking is following unwritten rules of the trail. If walking on a track at a YMCA or Wellness Center, walkers must stay to the right to allow runners to pass on the left. I rarely seek this type of walking since going around in circles offers no new vantages, and the noise from paired-walkers, basketball players, and weightlifters do not afford me the quiet and solitude to get lost in my thoughts, let alone lost on my path. Indoor, manufactured, walking tracks permit the walker to only go in one direction, and typically an arrow dictates whether that direction is clockwise or counter clockwise. Although one can choose which direction to take on the trail, the option is only two-fold. Outdoor manufactured trails also require walkers to stay on the right, and bicyclists announce their presence behind you by stating, "Passing on your left." Such declarations are appreciated when walking my dog to ensure I have her reined in to avoid being bound up in the spokes, but on more than one occasion these warnings have made me jump out of my deep contemplations. Thoreau would undoubtedly think of these walking trails as akin to bustling city streets where even the pedestrians must adhere to the rules of the road. "I do not travel in them (roads) much, comparatively, because I am not in a hurry to get to any tavern or grocery or livery-stable or depot to which they lead." (p. 16). I will admit, however, that having a destination in mind comforts my sense of order and completion. One cannot know when she has achieved her goal until one has been set. However, the destinations of our goals, like walking, can be varied and quickly altered.

Walking today is a social exercise. Thoreau would find this an atrocity. First, he believed walking was meant to be communing with nature and with your own thoughts. Second, "But the walking of which I speak has nothing in it akin to taking exercise." (p. 11). I was raised in a blue-collar household where exercise was synonymous with work. We did not exercise as a separate activity, but our physical labors provided a more comprehensive workout routine than any fitness center. Walking a mile each way to and from school is often thought a practice of living on the prairie, however, I walked two miles each school day from 1969-1980. Somedays it would be less as I cut through backyards and alleys. Despite my mother's admonitions that I was trespassing on people's properties, I never had anyone reprimand me, even when I stole an apple to nourish me on my walk home.

It comforts and saddens me to know that Thoreau faced the same dilemma I do: how to live a life of meaning and contribution. I am comforted that he simultaneously embraced civilization and tried to make it better through his teaching, his writing, and his work as an Abolitionist. I am saddened that over 150 years after his death, we are losing the wildness and the desire to become lost in our thoughts. "Hope and the future for me are not in lawns and cultivated fields, not in towns and cities, but in the impervious and quaking swamps." (p. 33). What will become of us a human race if we walk only for exercise and socializing on paved paths? I believe Thoreau was even disappointed with his own contemporaries for their lack of aimless wondering so I trust that he would be even more dismayed at our current attitude toward walking. While we could not have become a great nation without focused direction, I believe then, as now, that Thoreau would have urged his fellow humans to embrace the wildness of nature. Let that *wildness* beat throughout our beings and cause us to saunter toward a better understanding of our world and thereby be lightened through walking. "Alas for human culture! Little is to be expected of a nation, when the vegetable mould (sic) is exhausted, and it is compelled to make manure of the bones of its fathers." (p. 37).

Part Two

PANDORA: FIRST WOMAN or
30 MINUTES OF INTERNET RADIO

A Box

A box, like a heart,
Can hide and store
Our secrets and treasures.

A box, like a heart,
Should never be locked
Even for fear of breaking.

A box, like a heart,
Comes in all sizes
To be filled with memories.

Conjecture

Why this need to envision the future?
It will be here soon enough.

Forecasting the weather
To save a life
Anticipating a new life
To prepare for change
Foreseeing a change
To fix the faults
Adumbrating faults
To prolong the joy

Predicting winners
To make losing bearable
Foreshadowing the unbearable
To recognize the end
Prophesying the end
To a story where the last page is missing
Foreboding of all the memories that are missing
From the minds of those whose past
Is as unknown as the future.

A Bottle of Time

When the doctor announces you have a girl,
You praise God for 10 toes and 10 fingers.
When the doctor announces your 10-year-old girl has Crohn's,
You praise God it isn't that other C word.
When the doctor announces your 20-year-old girl has to have her colon removed,
You stand immobile in an empty pre-op room.
When the doctor announces your mother has two years to live,
You question your hearing because she's fought and won before.
When your mother asks you if we should bring in Hospice,
You deny the necessity because she's fought and won before.
When you ask the intensive care nurse, if your father can hold his wife while she dies,
You realize two years of denial has been a waste of time.

A Fine Girl

Her neighbors say, "Such a fine girl, so thoughtful to scoop my sidewalk."
Her parents say, "What a good girl, so respectful of her elders."
Her siblings say, "Such a goody-two-shoes."
Her teachers say, "What a smart girl. She'll go far."
Her doctors say, "What a courageous woman."
Her epitaph says, "A fine girl made her way through the world until she reached a dead end."

Breeze of Summer

Somehow we know it will be the last.
The last 4th of July picnic.
A picnic to bring four generations together one last time.
Time for food and boat rides and games.
Games to show we are alive and learning and facing the end.
The end will come when the breeze of summer gives way to the gales of December.

This has been going on for how long?

You've been having an affair?
You've been in college for how many years?
You've been stealing cable?
You borrowed my razor?
And my toothbrush?
You've been secretly living as a woman?
For what it's worth, I'm not surprised at any of it.

My Love's Best

I give my love the fattest chicken leg and the last piece of chocolate cake.
I give my love two beautiful children.
I give my love my compassion when the day has been long and disappointing.
I give my love the strength of my back that keeps a loving home to which he can return.
I give my love the freedom to pursue his dreams.
My love's best when not reciprocated
Means I give my love divorce papers.

Dreaming in California Soundbites

"I feel like we should be getting pedicures and watching *Beaches*."
"I like sex on the beach."
"I am short, but I'm not this short."
"I've gone home in a tablecloth before, you know."
"I have so many questions."
"I always feel like I look like a Christmas tree."
"Where is my fruit?"
"I'm not going to punch you in the face, Sir."
"I gave birth, and all I wanted was a cheese sandwich."
Why do celebrities only speak in first-person?

With You I Can Make IT

Information Technology
In-Training
Intergalactic Transportation
Ingrown Toenail
Inconsiderate Twaddle
Immaculate Transcendence

Sundown: An Original Poem by Pandora

"After a tequila sunrise,
Lady, here's
Your song.
She's gone.
Baby, come back.
Peg, in September
We've only just begun
Dancing in the Moonlight.
What a fool believes.
One of these nights Danny's song, Operator, but
That's not the way it feels.
I'd really love to see you tonight; let's stay together at least until
Saturday in the park.
Have you ever seen the rain?
Baby, I'm-a want you so
Take the long way home."

Delusions

Passengers of Flight 614 from Boise began to disembark. Nancy Campbell was among the first group to come down the ramp. Her petite frame was hidden behind a large woman loaded with Christmas presents, but as the group dispersed, Christina saw her mother.

"Mom!" Christina yelled. Then to Alicia, "Look, Sweet Pea, there's Grandma."

"Look at how big you are," said Nancy. "The last time I saw you, you were a pink, wrinkly bundle. How are you feeling?" This last question was directed to Christina.

"I'm fine, really," said Christina, but as always her response sounded curt.

"Well, you look wonderful. Personally, I think those doctors are lunatics. If you're feeling depressed, you pick yourself up."

"I know, Mom," said Christina. "Let's go get your bags."

"What's all the fuss?" Nancy asked when she finally managed to take in her surroundings. "Why all the cameras and reporters?"

"They're crowded around some man. I wonder if it's Raymond Williams. I heard on the news this morning he's arriving in Iowa today. I guess I never thought he might be on your flight."

"Oh, my goodness! I'm glad I didn't know that before. That man gives me the creeps, but looking at him now that his hair is long, you'd never know he's a White Supremacist."

"I think they labeled him a *separatist*, Mom, not a *supremacist*. Actually I feel a little sorry for the man. Both his wife and daughter killed, himself shot. His life will never be the same, and his reputation is ruined even if he was found innocent."

"Still. Living all that ways out in the woods, refusing any contact with others. I think that's a little strange. And it's completely absurd that the FBI had to apologize."

"Oh, I don't know. I think it would be kind of peaceful to live in a cabin up in the mountains. But enough about him, let's get your luggage and go home so you can play with your granddaughter."

Raymond Williams, a slight man wearing jeans and a Harley-Davidson t-shirt, had been making some observations of his own. His hair was slicked straight back emphasizing a face that was tanned and slightly weathered from years spent outdoors. He stood catatonic as his grey eyes focused on the woman holding the baby. "It's incredible," Ray thought to himself, "she looks exactly like Kristie, and the baby could be Alice. But that can't be. They've been dead for 14 months."

Ray wanted to follow them, but the reporters crowded around him as he started to move.

"Mr. Williams, now that you've been acquitted, are you going to file charges against the FBI for the wrongful deaths of your wife and daughter?" asked a reporter from the *Des Moines Register*.

"I don't think that's possible," returned Ray. "Right now I just want to see my two girls and spend Christmas with my family. If you'll excuse me, I want to get to my sister's house."

Walking down the concourse, Ray Williams, still intent on the woman and the baby, was followed by an entourage of media.

"Do you hold any grudges toward the U.S. government?" asked a reporter from Channel 8 News.

"I still don't really trust anything that has happened," began Ray. "The government is such a propaganda-spinning monster that it's hard to believe any of what it says."

"Does that mean you're not satisfied with the $3.1 million settlement from the Justice Department?"

"Would you trade your wife and daughter for three million dollars?" With that, Ray forced his way through them. He was glad he had convinced his sister not to bring his daughters to the airport. They had been through enough without seeing their own tear-stained faces on the six o'clock news. Somehow the fact that these would be tears of joy for the father they hadn't seen in six months held no consolation.

It was over. Why couldn't everyone just leave him alone? "Oh, God," Ray thought, "someone will probably make this into one of those damn, *made-for-T.V. movies*." Once again he was glad they didn't own a television set. Both he and Kristie didn't want the evils of society coming to them in their own living room. Yet evil had entered. Kristie and Alice had been shot by a sniper bullet while standing in that very living room.

After Christina claimed her mother's luggage, the three of them loaded into Christina's Jeep Cherokee. As she climbed behind the wheel, a man's voice stopped her.

"Excuse me. I just wanted to tell you how beautiful you are."

Turning around to offer a polite brush-off, she froze.

"You remind me of my wife. The two of you could be identical twins," said Ray.

"Aren't you Raymond Williams?"

A simple nod of his head forced Christina to stammer, "Your......wife......is......dead."

"That's what they said. But they've lied before."

"Christina, get in this car!" Nancy's stern voice brought Christina to her senses and, in what seemed one motion, she got into the car, locked the doors, turned the ignition, and squealed out of the parking space.

Ray didn't move. His eyes followed the Jeep through the toll booth, watched it turn right at the stop light, and drive out of sight.

"Can you believe it? I told you he was strange," Nancy said when the airport was out of sight. "Oh, it just makes me shiver. What did he say to you?"

Christina, still dazed, managed to relay to her mother what Ray had said to her. "Please don't tell Marcus, Mom. He'll just get upset and worry, and there's nothing he can do about it. Besides, Raymond Williams doesn't even now who I am, let alone where I live." "LXR832. Dallas County," Ray mumbled to himself. "Perhaps the government can help me after all."

Marcus and Christina had decided before Alicia was born that they did not want to raise their children in the city. Marcus's advertising job meant they had to stay close to Des Moines, but they chose to live in Woodward, a small town 30 minutes north of the city. They had bought a three-story Victorian that Christina was slowly restoring to its original splendor. She was currently working on turning the third floor into a playroom. Their bedrooms and Marcus's office were on the second floor, and the main living area occupied the first floor.

Christina quickly forgot about the episode with Ray as she busied herself with last-minute Christmas preparations. It would only be the four of them this year. Marcus was an only child, and his parents were spending the holidays in the Bahamas. Christina had a brother in Ohio, but he and his wife were expecting their second child any day. Nancy would be flying there after the New Year. They went to church on Christmas Eve and opened presents on Christmas morning. For her first Christmas, Alicia was more enthralled with the bows on the packages than with the treasures inside.

Christmas at the home of Patty Stephenson, Ray's sister, was not as joyous. "I wish Mommy and Baby Alice were here," cried Ruth, Ray's eight-year-old daughter.

"I know, Honey, I wish they were too. This would have been Alice's first Christmas. She would have loved all the ribbons and bows. Someday we'll all be together again." To himself Ray thought, "Maybe even sooner." But aloud he continued, "Now let's see what your Aunt Patty is doing in the kitchen." With that Ray scooped up his four-year-old daughter, Irene, and the three went to check on Christmas dinner.

"Did you call the airport about your luggage?" asked Patty as the reunited family entered.

"Yeah, they still haven't found it. As if they haven't done enough to my family, now they have to take away my babies' Christmas presents too. Why can't they just leave us alone?"

"The girls had the presents from me and Harold. It's not like they didn't have anything under the tree."

"You know what I mean."

Patty didn't know what her brother meant. In fact she was finding it more and more difficult to understand anything her brother said these days. Sometimes he talked like Kristie and Alice were still alive, and that the FBI had relocated them and changed their names. She had always admired her brother's pride and self-discipline and would always remember the day he finally returned from Vietnam. He had given her his green beret. Could these delusions stem from his 18 months of solitary confinement in a Cambodian POW camp? His VA therapist would say it was.

For Christina the day after Christmas was always a letdown. So much of the celebration was tied up in the preparation and anticipation that after it was over, there was emptiness. Emptiness that was heightened by two phone calls. The first, for Marcus, meant he would be leaving the next morning for Chicago. A client he had just acquired was not happy with the proofs and layouts Marcus had faxed before Christmas. Marcus needed to talk with them face-to-face to reassure them.

"I hate leaving you like this," said Marcus. "Are you sure you're going to be okay?"

Christina fought back the hurt. "Please don't worry. You don't need to look at me with such fear. The doctors have assured us that the Prozac is working. Alicia and I will be fine. Besides, Mom will be here if you feel you still can't trust me." The last statement was meant to sting.

With the second call they learned that Christina's brother and sister-in-law were the proud parents of an eight-pound, five-ounce baby boy, born that morning. Marcus and Nancy would both be leaving the next day.

Christina hid the hurt from the first phone call, but after the second call she retreated to the bathroom. Using the toilet as a chair, and with tissues in hand, she thought how depressing the holidays could be. Once again she worried that maybe the medication wasn't working. Sometimes if she forgot to take it, she became anxious and confused. One evening, about a month ago, Marcus had returned home to find Alicia in her crib screaming while Christina sat on the edge of the bed behind a locked door in their room next door. She had been paralyzed with fear that she would hurt Alicia because sometimes such horrible thoughts entered her mind. Once while drying the dishes, she picked up a knife and thought how easily she could silence Alicia if the crying didn't stop. The doctors had diagnosed it as depressive psychosis, a severe post-partum depression and had prescribed anti-depressant drug therapy. Without the medication she sometimes lapsed into such deep delusions that she couldn't even remember her own name.

****

The flights to Chicago and Cincinnati were three hours apart, and it seemed silly to make the 40-mile trip twice, so, after dropping Marcus off at the airport, Christina, Alicia, and Nancy headed for the mall. Nancy bought a layette sleeper with a matching receiving blanket, and Christina picked out a newborn baseball outfit. As she ran a finger down a blue pinstripe, she wondered if she and Marcus would have another baby. Could their relationship handle the strain of more accusations? Could she handle the doubts she felt about her motherly instincts and her sanity? Her mind raced to the previous summer. Walking with Alicia in the stroller, they were a few blocks from the park, when Christina was startled by a hand grabbing her shoulder.

"Christina, didn't you hear me? I've been hollering at you for the last block-and-a-half." It was her neighbor, Martha, but the only sounds she had heard were muffled and distant, yet she had sensed that someone was trying to penetrate the fog.

"Christina, did you hear me? I said it's ten o'clock. We'd better get back to the airport." It was Nancy's hand now that gently shook Christina's shoulder. "I want to get there early so I don't have to wait in line."

The parting was as tearful as the greeting had been, but Christina wasn't sure if the tears were for her Mother's departure or because she was now alone with her daughter. Christina and Alicia stood at the observation windows until the plane took off. "Look's like it's just you and me, Kiddo. Daddy won't be home until tomorrow night. What should we do?"

Christina expected no response and got none. Why was it, she wondered, that thoughts usually reserved for the mind could be verbalized in the presence of a baby? It was essentially just talking to yourself, but for some reason it wasn't considered insanity if you were holding a baby. She contemplated this as they walked down the concourse and passed the lost luggage claim's desk.

Ray couldn't believe his eyes. There she was. It was Kristie. She wasn't dead. And she had Alice with her. She hadn't seen him or even heard him calling her name, but then they had probably brainwashed her when they relocated her and changed her name. No longer worried about his lost luggage, Ray followed his lost love to put an end to this nightmare.

Traffic was light so it wasn't difficult for Ray to follow them in his sister's car. He didn't dare let Christina see him. Her reaction the other day was proof that they had succeeded in brainwashing her. "I'm glad they put them outside the city," Ray thought as they headed out of the city. "That's my Kristie. Stay away from the evils of society."

As she drove down Highway 141, Christina thought back to the first few months after Alicia was born. Marcus had been so cruel at times. When Alicia was about four months, he had insisted that they hire a nurse to live with them and help with the baby. Christina remembered a recurring argument.

"I don't trust her. She treats me like an invalid child. She's always looking over my shoulder when I hold Alicia. And I know she reports to you every night when you get home. I feel like a delinquent child whose probation officer is reporting to her father."

"Chrissy, you know you sometimes get confused and unsure of who or where you are. Do you remember when that photograph of Kristie Williams flashed across the television, you thought it was you. Christ, you didn't even believe I was your husband. For now you'll just have to trust that I know what's best."

"Kristie Williams." The name came rushing out of Christina's mouth and brought her back. "My God. Was it just a coincidence that Ray Williams approached me at the airport or did he really know me?" For the first time since Halloween, Christina questioned her own identity.

Ray followed as the Jeep took the Woodward State Hospital exit, but he held back. Every car is noticed in a small town. Fortunately she pulled into a driveway right off the main street enabling Ray to pull into the parking lot of the Woodchuck Inn two blocks away. For now he was on recon. He needed to be sure they hadn't set her up with a husband.

They didn't leave the house all day, and periodically Ray could see Christina through a third story window. She was wallpapering.

"That's my girl," Ray thought. "No sense wasting money on what you can do yourself. You can sense I've returned for you and Alice and now you're preparing our new home. I would've rather gone back to our cabin, but we can sell this house to follow our dream back in Idaho. Everything will come back to you once I've had a chance to remind you."

By eleven o'clock Ray felt confident no one else would be entering the house. With the stealth of a hunter, Ray headed for the Victorian house. As he crept onto the pillared-porch, he could see the blue, dancing light of a television being watched in the dark. He could see Christina sitting on the couch. He liked it when she wore her hair loose around her shoulders.

"I'm glad they didn't make you cut your beautiful hair," Ray whispered.

Silently he moved across the porch to the front door. The screen door was unlocked and rested on well-oiled hinges. The heavy wooden door, however, was locked. Ringing the bell wouldn't work, Ray thought, she wouldn't open the door when she saw it was him. There had been fear in her eyes the other day at the airport. Ray clenched his fists as he thought how an evil government had destroyed his life. First they made him think his wife and baby were dead, and then they stole his wife's past and his family's future. Did they figure since they couldn't get him on trumped-up charges of illegally selling firearms, they would resort to trickery? He would show them. He would reclaim what they had taken from him.

Ray walked to the rear of the house where he noticed a second story door that at one time had probably opened onto a veranda off the master bedroom. Scavenging through the garage, he found an extension ladder and crowbar. Gently he placed the ladder against the house. Like a panther creeping toward his prey, Ray climbed to the door and forced it open.

Christina turned off the television and stood in the darkness allowing her eyes to adjust before heading for the open staircase in the front foyer. As with most old houses, the stairs creaked. Christina welcomed this sound because it served as a reminder that no one could sneak up without being heard. "That includes Alicia when she is older," Christina smiled to herself.

Alicia's bedroom was at the top of the stairs and Christina entered it as she did every evening to make one last check of her sleeping child. Times like this she couldn't imagine how she could ever think of harming this innocent, helpless baby. The master bedroom was next door. Christina headed for the master bath first and clicked on the light. She brushed her teeth, put on her nightgown, and braided her hair into a loose plait. Clicking off the light, she didn't wait this time for her eyes to adjust but moved forward with outstretched arms until she felt the right poster of the oak bed frame. She pulled back the covers when a hand closed tightly over her mouth while the other clasped around her stomach forcing her arms tightly against her body.

"I'm sorry it has to be like this, Kristie," said Ray.

Christina froze, yet through the cloud of confusion, she thought the voice sounded familiar. "And what was that name he called me?" she thought. These random and fragmented thoughts raced through her mind. Another delusion? Had she remembered to take her medication?

"I've come back for you. I'm sorry for what they've done to you. I'm here now, and I'll never let them take you from me again." With this Ray swung Christina around so they were face-to-face. In that instant Ray removed his hand from her mouth and replaced it with his lips.

Christina's shock shifted to anger as she struck at him with her fists. She succeeded in breaking off the kiss but not in breaking his hold. She was now only a few inches from him and frantically searched her memory for some recollection.

"How I've missed touching your face and smelling your hair when your head rests on my shoulder. I want to hold you and never let you go."

"Ray? Raymond Williams?" She thought about screaming for help, but that would wake Alicia.

"Kristie. You recognize me. You know who I am. Say some more. I want to hear your voice. It's been so long I hardly remember it."

"Why do you keep calling me Kristie? My name is *Christina*. The only person who ever called me Kristie was my father, and he's been dead for five years."

"Your given name is *Kristine*, but I've always called you *Kristie*, ever since high school."

"We never went to high school together. Why are you here? What do you want?"

"Listen to me carefully. Here, let's sit down on the bed. The government has brainwashed you. You are my wife. We have three daughters: Ruth, Irene, and Alice. We used to live in a cabin on Diamond Bluff in Idaho. You had a vegetable and herb garden behind the cabin. Can you remember any of this?"

"You're insane. I left Idaho after I graduated from high school." Christina leapt toward the door, but Ray grabbed her around the waist and tackled her to the floor.

"I don't expect you to believe this all at once. Your memories will probably come back in bits and pieces. For now, you'll just have to trust that I know what's best."

"Trust you? You've got to be kidding. That's what you said when you hired the nurse." Christina's mind was racing. No, that wasn't him. Marcus had said that. No longer sure of anything, Christina screamed, "Help! Help me, someone!"

Ray thrust his hand over her mouth. "Quiet, Kristie, you'll wake the baby. I guess until I can convince you, I'll have to restrain you. I don't want to do this, but as usual the government has forced me to do things I don't want to do. Please forgive me, Kristie."

Ray took out his handkerchief and tied it over Christina's mouth. Using the curtain tie-backs, he tied her hands and feet to the four posters of the bed.

"It's been a long time," Ray whispered as he knelt on the floor near her head. "So many nights I've laid awake remembering how wonderful it was to make love to you. Can I make love to you now?"

Christina whimpered, shaking her head back-and-forth, pulling her legs together in futile desperation.

"I know you're frightened, but this might help you remember."

Ray walked to the foot of the bed and slowly pushed the blue satin nightgown up toward Christina's chest.

Slowly and silently the bedroom door opened.

Again Christina whimpered and thrashed as Ray mounted her.

"Chrissy? What's wrong? What's going on?"

This time there was no fog, no echoing sounds from the distance. Christina recognized this voice immediately and let out muffled screams.

Marcus rushed toward the bed, toward the heap hovering over his wife. With his hands clasped and raised above his head, Marcus bludgeoned Ray's back. Ray toppled down onto Christina, but Marcus quickly grabbed him by the collar and swung him around. With the momentum of being swung around, Ray landed a right hook to Marcus's jaw. Marcus reeled backwards but came back with a head butt to Ray's stomach causing both men to tumble to the floor. Marcus took this wrestling advantage and put his knees on Ray's arms, pinning him. Again and again Marcus pummeled Ray's face until he felt the body go limp. He lifted himself off Ray and hurried to untie Christina.

"Don't touch her. She's mine," yelled Ray as he lunged toward Marcus, who had only succeeded in untying Christina's right hand.

It was now Ray who had the advantage of a surprise attack. He threw Marcus against the mirrored dresser and then against the closet door. Air rushed from Marcus's lungs as Ray put an elbow to his stomach. When Marcus doubled-over, Ray followed with an uppercut. In the next instant Ray's hands were around Marcus's neck. Marcus was losing his footing and sliding down the closet door. His head felt congested. He couldn't focus his eyes. "Is that Alicia crying?" he wondered. He heard a crash. "Alicia's fallen out of her crib? Get her Chrissy." But the words wouldn't form.

In the next instant air rushed back into his lungs. Christina was leaning over him, her voice soothing. He looked over her shoulder and saw the shattered mirror on the floor next to Ray's body.

"It's over. No more delusions. I know who I am," Christina whispered.

Looking into his wife's eyes, Marcus allowed a wry smile to curve his lips as he said, "Honey, I'm home."

PART THREE

APHRODITE: GODDESS OF LOVE AND BEAUTY

To Botox or Not to Botox

To Botox or not to Botox? Is that really a question?
Whether 'tis nobler in the mind to
Suffer the lines and furrows of life's misfortunes
Or to take a needle against the advancing war of age,
And by attempting to turn back time
Render our faces immobile, and in being expressionless end
Our ability to extend a smile of friendship or the
Look of disgust that is but intrinsic
To the very heart of what makes us human!
To Botox, perchance to recapture youth's glow – ay, that's the catch,
For to appear young is what our society deems beautiful
When in fact, it should be the wisdom of the aged
That gives us pause to think how disrespectful
We are to these hard-fought badges of tenacity.

Fleeting Moments

Crab apple blossoms
Lilacs
Time spent with Mom
A baby's room
Pomp and circumstance
A marching band
Christmas Eve
Worry
A good night's sleep
Feeling forlorn
Summer storms
A silent phone
Fleeting moments
Briefly alive
Most melt into memory
Even before they pass
Quickly they scurry
Living life in a hurry

Wink at the Moon

I wink at the moon for it knows my secret.
Its full, round face illuminates my tear.
Its brightness subdues the ache in my heart,
From wishing you were here.
There are no stars for wishing,
And it wouldn't be fair, I fear.
For wishing would keep you here with me
And not with your Father dear.

I sometimes hear your voice amid
the falling and waking hours.
I sometimes see you standing among
the growing and dying flowers.
I sometimes smell your fragrance afresh
in warm summer showers.
I sometimes feel your touch atop
my hand to instill your powers.

The moon knows all this from a tear and a wink
How I hate that you're missing my life.
Is that selfish? Am I on the brink?
Well, I'm tired of playing the brave heart
With a quick smile and a faster blink
Because it's too far past the mourning time
For public signs of grief, so I must shrink
From the pain that only the moon knows.

I loathe the cancers that robbed you of life
From being a mother, grandmother, and wife.
I want to scream at the moon like a blaring fife
But instead I wink at the moon so I don't feel the knife

Thrust toward the depths of my strife.
My mother is dead, and the moon hears my bewailing
It sees my wink and sends my secret sailing
Toward the morning sun where promise is never failing.

The "C" Word

There is a place I don't want to go
In my mind
A place where my daughters have
No mother
If the remission ends again
A place where I succumb
To the fear
Can't say the word
Speaking makes it real
Keep busy
Keep moving
Keep living

Of Love and Like

In my dreams miles do not separate us.
There is only the distance
From my hand to yours
From your heart to mine.
When we are together, days sprout wings.
When we are apart, hours are an anchor
Weighing heavy on my heart.

The sweetness of your smile,
The gentleness of your touch,
The attentiveness of your heart,
The patience of your soul,
For these things I love you, but
More importantly
Because of these, I like you.

The Brave and His Bride

The wind whispered as I stood on the side of the hill and
Felt the spirit of every creature who had passed here before.
Their breath the wind
Their bodies the trees
Their tears the river

Leaves jostled in tiny whirlwinds about the ground
Echoing former footsteps that once
Stood in this clearing
"Who are you?" I asked, but
They scurried deeper into the woods

I imagined it was a brave returning from battle
Meeting his anxious bride
Their breath catching
Their bodies entwined
Their tears of joy

Seasoned Encounters

Salt and Pepper lived in the cupboard by the stove.
As an integrated social unit, they were never just one or the other, but
Always Salt-n-Pepper, together.
They relished how each brought something unique to the table.
Salt had the uncanny ability to draw-out the flavor in all she met.
Pepper knew how to spice even the dullest of parties.

All was harmony for Salt and Pepper until one day
Pepper realized Salt was leaving the cupboard more and more and
Staying away longer and longer. Upon returning,
Salt was always used and empty, too tired for cooking.
Did people like Salt better?
Despite receiving top-billing on the spice rack, Pepper noticed colors and was intrigued.

"Too much of you, Salt, is bad for people.
You can cause them to stroke-out.
No one has ever died from eating too much of me."

"Maybe not, Pepper, but too much of you makes people sneeze.
They throw you down in disgust.
People always assume you'll make their noses run."

"It's not their noses that will run but their blood pressure if they run to you."

"I can't live like this any longer. I'm going to live with my cousin, Sea Salt, in Aruba."

"What do I care? I've found true passion with Mrs. Dash and her many, lovely colors.
She will forever be my one-and-only, monosodium glute-a-mate. "

I Thought About You Less Today

I thought about you less today than I did the day before.
Thought less about the way you coaxed my feelings and stimulated my mind.
Thought less about the intensity of your gaze that penetrated my soul.
Thought less about our hikes and meetings for coffee and drinks.
Thought less about subtle touches and glances before I even knew you were there.

I thought about you less today than I did the day before, and the day before that.
Thought less about your pursuit of me until I realized too late what I had lost.
Thought less about your casual passing by my door to stay for an hour's chat.
Thought less about your phone calls and text messages that made my heart race.
Thought less about the snowstorm that we drove through just to be together.

I thought about you less today than I did the day before, and the day before that, and the day before that.

Forego or Reclaim

Will the footfalls of former lovers force me to forego these trails, or shall I reclaim the fallen trees along the winding creek?

Must I forego the comforts of my refuge until the echoes of flirtation subside, or shall I reclaim my muse with a resounding shout, "I am free to love again"?

Am I destined to forego the leaf-strewn paths to plod along the skirting road above, or shall I reclaim the only lover who has never abandoned me?

Shall I follow your resilience and awaken again and again and again, no matter how many times winter's clutches tear my heart?

Shall I plunge deep into your ravine until the sunlight is spotted across my closed lids, or retreat to inner chambers and be lost behind drawn curtains?

Forego and forfeit existence.
Reclaim and risk everything.

Excalibur

Never love,
Never lose.
Never let you in,
Never languish.
Never too close to break.
Sun on the outside.
Stone on the inside.
Holding fast to Excalibur.
Hoping hard someone has
Skill to grab the hilt.

Vigilant

Surely as humans disappoint the gods,
We disappoint ourselves and each other
For not being
Venturous
Inspired
Gracious
Inspiring
Loving
Accessible
Natural
Tolerant
Enough.

Ahamen Settlement

The *Century Farm* plaque was the last memory Adeline grabbed before walking toward their rust-pocked pickup. She had been raised on this land as had her father and grandfather before her. Her great grandfather, Johann, had settled on the Iowa farmland after emigrating from Germany in the late 1800's. He had escaped famine to bring his family of 14 to the land of plenty and opportunity. Now Adeline, her husband Henry, and their 10 children were being evicted, forcibly removed from the only home she and her children had ever known. She stilled her mind and thought fondly of the stories Opa Johann had told of being one of the earliest settlers to break the virgin soil.

"Come here, my sweet, little Adeline and let your old Opa tell you about this land." Even at the young age of four, Adeline felt a bond toward the land. "The prairie grass was as high as your head," he continued, "and the color of your chestnut hair." Taking her plaited hair, he would show her how he guided the oxen with his gentle voice and slight tugging of the reins. "Back then we used our livestock for work and food. Now your papa feeds them until they are fat enough to sell again at market." Adeline could envision herself atop Opa's oxen more easily than sitting on the wheel cover of her father's new John Deere.

A crack of thunder caused Adeline to gather her children into the pickup like a mother goose guiding her goslings to shelter. They were headed for the Ahamen Settlement in Nebraska. The older children climbed into the bed of the truck atop boxes and furniture, which were all that remained of a half-century of living on this land. The rest of the household items and all the machinery would be sold at auction, the profits going to replant those chestnut-colored grasses.

Chief White Cloud fired a shot into the air. At first Adeline thought it was another crack of thunder until she saw through the side-view mirror, the red-skinned man approaching the truck and reloading his rifle. She urged her husband, Henry, to head the truck down the long lane. White Cloud's men would be waiting at the end of it to escort them to Ahamen, picking up other farm families along the way. Moving toward uncertainty, her mind returned to the certitude of youth.

"Weren't you scared, Oma Ella?" a young Adeline asked her great grandmother. The little girl loved to hear the story of how her ancestors traveled to Iowa in prairie schooners. As she practiced her needlepoint, she could see them in the distance, the prairie grass hiding the wagon wheels, transforming the wagon train into a fleet of white-sailed vessels carrying home and hope.

"Yes, I was scared," answered Ella, "but I was with my family. That was all I cared."

The thought of family brought Adeline back to her four eldest sons sitting atop boxes in the bed of the truck, backs straight, chins high, eyes glaring ahead. The only gift she and Henry had ever been able to give their children was pride in their hard work. Work that should have seen the farm passed on to them. Adeline feared that such pride would now make their reclassification more difficult. Once they reached Ahamen, all the children would be sent to the Native Man's school. No longer allowed to wear jeans, boots, and caps, they would be forced to wear the Native Man's clothes. The Ahamen School would force them to read stories about Chief Black Hawk and Sitting Bull, heroes of the Native Man's people but strangers to her children. She shuddered at what her Opa and Oma would think of her children going to church without cleanly shorn heads and wondered again if the Native Man would even allow them to worship their God as they had always done.

Adeline thought of the white-steepled church amongst corn and bean fields that had christened, married, and buried three generations. She would no longer visit and decorate the graves of her ancestors. With the faith of a farmer, Adeline had sat in that church for 59 years praying. Praying for rain. Praying the hail wouldn't damage the crops. Praying for sunshine. Praying for the rain to stop before the spring seedlings were drowned. What god would the Native Man make them pray to?

"And what of her dear Henry," feared Adeline. A farmer all his life, he would be retrained to hunt for their food and provide the hides Adeline and her daughters would have to work into clothing, blankets, and shelter. What would they do for money? The new ethanol plant had finally allowed Henry to make a profit from his corn crop, but the plant had been the first obstacle removed by the Native Man. Adeline knew that the fossil fuels used faithfully by her father and grandfather would be gone by the time Adeline's baby reached middle age, but without the ethanol and coal and nuclear plants there would be no electricity for their homes and no fuel for their truck. Everything they had known and done and been would be gone. The weight of her ancestors came crashing down upon her.

As they neared the end of the lane, Adeline soothed herself with knowing she and the other farm women at the Ahamen Settlement would be allowed to grow the gardens she had always treasured. The smile that had been absent from her lips for the last several months returned as she thought, "Perhaps someday my great grandchildren will return to Iowa floating on a prairie schooner."

By the time they reached Sioux City, a caravan of 900 families trudged toward the uncertainty awaiting them on the Nebraska flat lands. Adeline reread the Native Man's letter informing them the land of her ancestors was no longer hers. It spoke of the Ioway Treaty of 1854 that ceded all lands to the United States with all monies made from the sale of those lands to be given to the Ioway. Now, after 150 years, the Native Man had convinced the Great White Father in Washington that an important part of this treaty had not been respected. Adeline read aloud, "Until after the said land shall have been surveyed, and the surveys approved, no white persons or citizens shall be permitted to make thereon any location or settlement." The White Man now admitted that no surveys of the Ioway territory had ever been recorded. Furthermore, the Ioway's had received no money. The White Man had no rights to the Iowa land. All White Men in the land between the Missouri and Mississippi had to leave.

As tears again threatened to spill, Adeline let the letter slip from her lap. She stared at it lying at her feet, a message that separated hearts from roots. Looking at it upside down, she let the word *Ahamen* burn into her brain until, in the voice of Opa Johann, she heard the word *Nemaha. Nemaha. Nemaha.* Nemaha Reservation.

She knew it now. The place the White Man had made for half-breeds and outcasts, the Native Man now used to retrain them.

Opa Johann had taken pity on those lost souls being sent to Nemaha and had hired two of them as farmhands. One man, John Little Wolf, wanted to learn to read and write, and Oma Ella worked with him after chores. Adeline had only met Little Wolf once when she was six, but she could still see those piercing grey eyes that reminded her of a ghost.

Adeline snatched the letter from the pickup floor. It couldn't be. The signature. The man who had convinced the Great White Father and argued before the White Man's Supreme Court was John L. Wolfe. "Dear God," Adeline prayed, "please visit this man's heart and plant in him the memory of my great grandfather who gave his great grandfather a second chance. And please plant in him the memory of my great grandmother who taught his great grandfather to read and write so he could inspire his great grandson to go to law school. Please, Dear Father, grant that this man will take pity on my family and educate them and teach them patience so that one day my great grandson can reclaim his birthright."

Adeline wrapped the Native Man's letter around her family's Century Farm plaque. This time would be different. This time they would get it right.

Part Four
ATHENA: GODDESS OF WISDOM

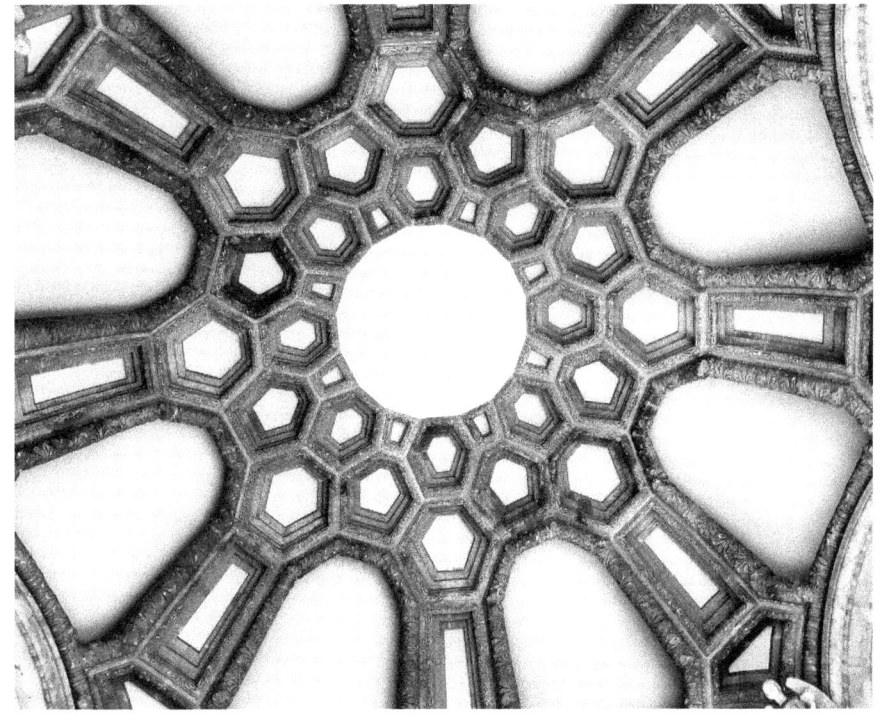

Journals of my Youth

I found the journals of my youth and was
Swept away on waves of angst and
Possibility.
Great courage was needed to look
Back at the person I was, to
Read words about the person
I had hoped to become
Now that I am the woman I am.
Pages devoted to
New love
Lost love
All these years later and
No wiser.
Old journals should come with warning labels
"Enter at the risk of discovering
That nothing has changed."

Becoming my Mother

I've started collecting napkins, paper towels, and tissues
In pockets, on countertops, and my desk.
People tell me I look like her.
I certainly hear her voice each time I
Call with a lilting voice,
"Hellooooo, I'm hooome."
It's only fitting then that I start to take on her
Little habits like wearing work clothes until they're
Truly dirty because working outside in clean clothes
Seems silly.
My daughters laugh and jibe.
I smile and nod and say,
"Just wait. Someday you'll become your mother."

Anomaly

If a picture paints a thousand words,
then who will care to read my words
when they could gaze upon ten pictures and thus
add ten thousand words to their vocabularies
that will never be used to describe a single picture?

What if.....

What if....
......having a thick skin was literal
And every time we sacrificed, or
Were humiliated or hurt,
We lost a layer?
Unlike a skinned knee that heals,
The silent pains would eat away the layers year by year.
Thus the translucent skin of the aged
Appears like the jelly fish
Exposed
Surrendered

What if.....
.....eating your words was nutritious
And every barb and slander were swallowed instead of spoken?
Unlike food with calories,
We would actually lose weight
By refusing to utter words that cut and slice
Another's character and morale.
Learning to swallow rather than spit
Would warrant a thick skin unnecessary, and
Make obesity
Obsolete

For You, I Wept

I wept for you.
I did not know you, yet I wept for you.
I wept for the sunshine you will never feel
For the stars you will never see
For the family you will never know.

I wept for you.
For your first day of school
For your skinned knees and skinned hearts
For the days of frolic and mischief
Vacant from your dreams.

I wept for you.
For your first date, first kiss, first prom
For all the avenues your life could have followed
For the waste of possibilities,
Stunted before the start.

I wept for me.
For the loss I feel in not knowing you
For the changes you could have brought
To a world smoldering in contempt
For my own shortcomings
Made manifest by your short life,
I wept.

The Test

Never before have I felt the confines of radical extremists in my own community.
Never before have I been afraid to speak out for fear of persecution.
Never before have I felt so vastly different from my neighbors.
Never before have I felt as if I were living in a foreign land, not understanding the rhetoric of my own people.

My stomach heaves.
My heart has taken-up
Permanent residence in my throat.
I have failed the test.

I had been confident that had I been alive during WWII, I would've supported the plight of the Jews.
I had been confident that had I been old enough during Vietnam, I would've protested in the streets.
I had been confident that had I been given the chance to jump on the bus, I would've been a Freedom Rider.
I had been confident that had I been richer, I could've helped the plight of the poor.

I had the opportunity to place a sign in my yard, take a stand, spout my beliefs,
But I feared retaliation from the small-minded demographic that put him in office.
"I have to live and teach in this town," I justified, so
I stumped loudly with like-minded friends.
As much as I despise him and am confused by his followers, They did what I could not.
Placed signs in their yards, stickers on their cars, and badges on their chests.

Never again shall I be confident in my own ferocity to stand for **my ideals.**
I was faced with a test,
and I failed.

Adventures

Sometimes an adventure is as simple as
driving a different route to work or
walking your dog on a new trail.

Sometimes an adventure is as simple as
reading a new book or
watching an old movie with younger eyes.

Sometimes an adventure is as simple as
listening instead of speaking or
saying *yes* when you always say *no*.

I Blame The Walkman

I blame the Walkman
For creating a generation that gave birth to a generation
Oblivious to their surroundings
Afraid of silence
Ignorant of where their thoughts might lead them.

All-Knowing

A caring person would say
Put an end to poverty
A learned person would say
There can be no wealth without poverty.
A tolerant person would say
We must accept all beliefs
A wise person would say
There can be no acceptance without denial.
A patient person would say
Change takes time
A discerning person would say
There are different times relative to where you are.
An intuitive person would say
I understand where you're coming from
A reasoned person would say
There can be no understanding without questioning.
Must the caring, tolerant, patient, intuitive person
Be pitted against the learned, wise, discerning, reasoned person, or
Can it be all-for-one and one-for-all?

It's a Crying Day

It's a crying day wrapped in sunflowers.
   The pain is everywhere, and the reality that you're dying
      Washes over me in showers
         Of sadness, bitterness, and guilt.

Did I tell you
   Did I show you
      That your love and friendship cover me like a patchwork quilt

Whose squares tell the story of a life bursting
   With colors only your eyes could invent
      On a palette fresh
         To paint a life still thirsting

3 of 99

I looked toward the blue sky above the white snow and
Thanked God and
Allah and
The Great Spirit for blessing me.
As I finished my thanks,
First one bird,
Then another, and
Finally another
Flew past my line of sight.
Each taking my praise of
Merciful One,
Forgiving One, and
Patient One to
God
Allah
Great Spirit.

The Crown

I have resisted this very act for it gives voice to
Fears, anxieties, uncertainties.
The fields and lakes care not,
The geese and deer know not
For I have always practiced social distancing with them.
To be the water gently caressing the rocks
Touch is connection
Connection is life
Life is fragile
The very reason for these fears, anxieties, uncertainties.
The Crown has traveled thousands of miles
To connect us all

Gehenna

Jezereen hated the days when it was her turn to venture outside the walls of the city to the garbage dump. She was afraid. Afraid that the very bowels of hell would reach a skeletal hand and drag her to the depths of she knew not what. It was on these days when she dragged her family's refuse to the dump that she understood how ignorance bred fear. She had been going to the Gehenna Garbage Dump now for three years, ever since the 12th year of her existence, and nothing remotely scary had happened to her. She had seen plenty of rotting flesh, and today she stared wide-eyed as the worms crawled in and out of what appeared to have been a man's ear a month earlier. She knew she should have looked away, but the sheer grotesqueness of the white worms crawling out of the white skull had fixed her eyes until the sulfur smell brought the tears and reminded her that Mother had told her to come straight home after going to Gehenna.

As Jezereen walked home, she wondered what that man had done to get himself killed and thrown on the garbage heap. There were so many men these days who were hanged or stoned for the smallest of offenses. Her own brother, Thomas, two years her elder, wasn't allowed to leave the house for fear that he would look improperly at someone who would report him to the authorities. Jezereen's family and everyone in her city lived in fear now, not just from the Gehenna but from what had recently happened in New Sodom. Her mother reminded everyone daily how her cousin Joshua had perished in that disaster, and the same fate could befall them. One of Jezereen's classmates, Michael, had been sent home from school for patting another boy on his bottom. He said they were just playing around, but the principal insisted on sending him home. It had been a month now, and he hadn't returned to school. Could it be his bones on which the white worms now feasted? She wondered even harder why the hands of hell hadn't dragged his body down so they could pick on his flesh rather than leave it to the white worms. Michael was one of the few boys Jezereen's age that her brother Thomas liked and didn't mind when he hung around their home. She wondered if she should tell Thomas about the white worms and ask him if he thought it might be Michael. As if her thoughts conjured him, Thomas rounded the corner of their house.

"What are you doing outside?" Jezereen asked her brother.

"Jezzie, you startled me. I can't stay hidden like a bastard child. I need fresh air. I need to be around people other than you and Mother and Father," Thomas replied. "I'll go crazy if I stay inside much longer. Please don't tell Mother that you saw me."

"Alright. But please be careful." Jezereen wondered and worried if it was wise to let him go. She would be punished if her parents knew she had seen Thomas leave the house and didn't tell them. But she couldn't betray her brother's trust, and she had promised. She decided the best course would be to follow him and keep an eye on him. He was probably just going down to the river to skip some stones and have a swim. She stayed well behind him and off the main path because he was looking all around him as if searching for something. Jezereen took to a side-path and started to cut directly to the river when she noticed Thomas had turned off toward the Gehenna. If he wanted some fresh air that certainly wasn't the place to get it, she thought. She was about to yell out to him when she saw another boy come out from behind some bushes. The boy looked like Michael, and she almost came out from her own bushes when she saw the two of them embrace. In the same way her eyes had fixed on the white worms, Jezereen stood motionless watching her brother kiss Michael square on the mouth. Thomas took a package out from under his shirt and gave it to Michael who ravenously unwrapped it and devoured its contents. Jezereen recognized the half-eaten sandwich that Thomas had told their mother he was too full to eat at lunch. She could keep silent no longer.

As she stepped out onto the open path, Michael dropped the sandwich to the dust, and in a barely audible gasp said, "Jezzie. Please don't tell anyone." He was about to run away when Thomas grabbed his arm and held him fast.

"What have you seen, Jezzie?" asked Thomas.

"Enough to know that Michael isn't the body I saw on the garbage heap this morning and that you'll both soon be joining whose ever body it was."

"Why? Why does this have to be wrong?" Michael had again found his voice, undoubtedly buoyed by Thomas's touch.

"I don't understand, Michael," Jezereen wondered. "I thought the Elders had killed you or sent you away for touching that boy."

"That's what the Elders want everyone to think. They want you to believe that they kill people they feel are unclean. They tell everyone that they stone us and throw our bodies into the Gehenna, but really they take us to a cave in the hills behind the city where they make us do exactly what they accuse us of."

"If I hadn't followed him the night they took him away," Thomas added. "He would be chained there with the rest of them right now."

"Won't the Elders come looking for you?" Jezereen asked.

"Why would they? They know I can't return to the city," said Michael.

"So you hide here in the Gehenna because you know no one will come looking for a living person here," said Jezereen.

"It won't be for much longer," said Thomas. "Tonight I'm going to take the money Mother and Father have hidden in the house so we can run away."

"You're insane. Where will you go? Every city and village has a Gehenna with fires that burn constantly."

"There are places where we will be accepted and welcomed," said Thomas. "Places where we're not cast out to live among the refuse. Some of the other boys talk about a place called New Valhalla where everyone lives in peace, and there is no Gehenna."

"Were you just going to leave without telling me?" Jezereen wondered.

"I would've written you a letter in a few months, maybe a year. Whenever we were settled," said Thomas.

"What if I don't approve of what the two of you are doing?" she asked.

"I'm still your brother. Do you love me less for being made as I am? Would you rather see me tossed aside just as you toss our family's garbage into Gehenna?"

Coming down the path were two young girls carrying their families' garbage. Michael returned to his hiding place. Thomas grabbed his sister's arm and with downcast eyes headed them both toward home. With but a slight glance backward, Jezereen met Michael's frightened eyes.

www.ingramcontent.com/pod-product-compliance
Lightning Source LLC
Chambersburg PA
CBHW060406050426
42449CB00009B/1915